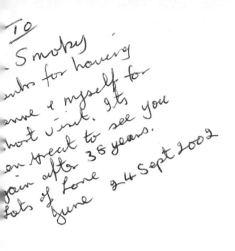

TO

Smoky

thanks for having
anne & myself for
a short visit. Its
an treat to see you
again after 35 years.
Lots of love
June   24 Sept 2002

Gravesend
in old picture postcards

Douglas W. Grierson

European Library ZALTBOMMEL / THE NETHERLANDS

GB ISBN 90 288 5747 8

© 1993 European Library – Zaltbommel/The Netherlands

Fifth edition, 2000: reprint of the original edition of 1993.

European Library

post office box 49

NL – 5300 AA Zaltbommel/The Netherlands

telephone: 0031 418 513144

fax: 0031 418 515515

e-mail:publisher@eurobib.nl

INTRODUCTION

Gravesend, recorded as Gravesham in the Domesday Book in 1086, is situated in Kent, 22 miles from London on the southern shore of the River Thames. The name Gravesend often provokes doubts as to its origin. It has nothing to do with the plague or graves, but is thought to derive from the Anglo-Saxon 'graafe' or 'reeve'. 'Graves ham' would be the graafe's home and another possibility is 'greave', meaning woods. The name altered to Gravesend and remained so until the new Borough of Gravesham was formed in 1974, adopting the original Domesday Book name.

Gravesend offers the first landing place or 'hythe' for passengers and shipping, travelling up the River Thames and is on the old road between London and Dover.

The population of Gravesend and Milton was 9,445 in 1831 and increased over the next 100 years to 35,490. The largest increase was during the ten years between 1831 to 1841, when the population rose by 6,215. During the early years of the 19th century, Gravesend was a popular place for visitors. In 1815, the first steamer arrived, building up a regular traffic between Gravesend and London, which was previously carried out by tilt boats.

The Town Pier was opened in 1834, despite a riot by watermen during the construction, and an estimated 300,000 passengers travelled between Gravesend and London.

The railway from London arrived in 1849, and the improving attractions of the Kent coast meant a decline in the number of visitors.

In 1900, Duncan Moul, in his handbook 'Weekends in Dicken's Land', wrote the following about Gravesend:

'The town is a busy thriving place, not very interesting or beautiful at first glance, but, like most places, it will pay for investigation, and has played its part in the history of the nation.' A statement true to this day.

Much of old Gravesend has vanished, either by vast slum clearances or by redevelopment of sites along the river front. The countryside and agricultural land to the south and south-east of the borough has been lost through extensive residential development.

The Borough of Gravesend was incorporated by charter during the reign of Queen Elizabeth I in 1567, and again in 1568, being renewed and extended in 1632. Several acts of Parliament in the late 19th and early 20th centuries, increased the size of Gravesend. By 1935, included in the Borough were Ifield, the Parishes of Denton and Chalk, and parts of Cobham and Northfleet. The local government act of 1974 incorporated Gravesend into the Borough of Gravesham, along with Northfleet and part of Strood Rural District Council (Higham, Shorne, Cobham and Luddesdowne, Meopham and Harvel).

The unique position of Gravesend meant that the principal industry of the town was connected with the river and shipping.

'A marine watering place, equal, if not superior, in point of attraction and economy to any other in the United Kingdom.' Tourism during the 19th century, provided the town with a substantial seasonal income and theatres, pleasure gardens, hotels and guest houses, public houses and refreshment houses blossomed for the benefit of the numerous visitors from London. By 1891, Gravesend had over ninety hotels, inns and public houses. Attractions in and around Gravesend included the following: the Victoria Tea Gardens, Clarke's Nurseries, Rosherville Gardens, Clifton Marine Baths, Windmill Hill, Tivoli Gardens, Tulleys Bazaar, the Literary Institute, the Terrace Gardens, Springhead Gardens and the Promenade. The total number of passengers to Gravesend by river exceeded 1,000,000 per annum in the 1840's.

The military importance of the location of Gravesend is seen by the establishment of the blockhouses and the fort to protect London and the upper reaches from invasion. Gravesend was the embarkation and arrival point for thousands of soldiers to and from the British Empire and conflicts. The emigrant ships in the River Thames meant that Gravesend was the last town they set foot on in England. This floating community was attended to by the towns clergy. The Customs and Excise Service were needed to observe and check the shipping from all over the world. Royal visitors were frequently using the Royal Terrace Pier to arrive and depart. Expeditions and explorers left from here on their way to different parts of the world. Charles Dickens visited and stayed in Gravesend, spending his honeymoon in Chalk village. Eventually he ended up living not far away, at Gads Hill, Higham, until his death.

In 'Caddells Guide to Gravesend' of 1818, the author states: 'It will be said, perhaps, that the inhabitants of Gravesend shew little desire of public distinction, since they take so little pains to obtain it; and that they so entirely neglect the unequalled capabilities of their situation.' I hope what is left of Gravesend, will remain and improve-ments kept in sympathy. The comments refer to the appearance of the town and the lack of accommodation for visitors. They were also directed at the council for the lack of water-carts to dampen the main road and thereby reducing the amount of dust blowing about during the summer, creating a discreditable nuisance.

With much of old Gravesend now gone, I hope you will enjoy the photographs and postcard views in this book. All have come from my own collection and I have limited the area of the views to the pre-1935 borough. A special thanks must go to Robert Hiscock, for suggesting that I undertake this task, and to my parents, for saving my early postcards and supporting this hobby.

I dedicate this book to my wife Doreen and my two sons, Simon and Ben, all born in Gravesend.

About the author

A former Metropolitan and Kent police officer, I married into the Solomon family, where I have been a funeral director for the past 16 years. I am a member of the Gravesend Historical Society and the Kent Archaeological Society. Family history research, coupled with the early interest in postcards, developed into a finding out more about the local history of Gravesend, Northfleet and the surrounding villages. This has evolved into giving numerous lectures and displays to various local societies and organisations.

1. *The earliest commercial photographs* of Gravesend were probably the 'carte de visite' views of shipping off Gravesend, taken by Frederick C. Gould, photographer of 10 Harmer Street, Gravesend, established in 1855. Gould would take photographs of the ships and produce them fairly quickly forsale as souvenirs. The card shown, is of the S.S. Orient, c. 1880, and the reverse shows a number of different ship photographs available. The list contained 45 ships, including an earlier S.S. Lusitania and the S.S. Great Britain. Many of Goulds photographic plates are in the National Maritime Museum. The 'carte' views cost 7d and the larger prints, mounted on card, 2/6 each.

2. *Prolific* with the visitors to and inhabitants of Gravesend were the number of photographic studios offering their services. Some photographers offered their services at Windmill Hill in order to catch the visitors. Nicholson, 'at the foot of Windmill Hill', Whateller, 'Union Street and the top of Windmill Hill'. The established photographers in the town were Gould, Willis, Honey, Hider, Edwards and later Munns, who also produced postcards. This photograph, a cabinet print, by A. Honey & Co, 3 Windmill Street, Gravesend, is of a boy in a huge frilly shirt, wearing knickerbockers and accompanied by a dog.

3. *Fletcher's wharf*, looking along Clifton Marine Parade, c. 1900. The tracks are for the chalk trucks, clearly visible, with sailing barge alongside. Piles of flints lie to the right. Mr. Fletcher lived at 'Bycliffes' near to the wharf. The wharf was originally Ditchburn's New Wharf. He was a chain- and ropemaker and mayor of Gravesend. The wharf was then purchased by William Gladdish, who used it for providing the ballast in coal schooners, returning to the River Tyne. The building close by, is the 'Hit or Miss' public house, named either after a former bowling green nearby or after the shooting range in the chalk pits behind. In the distance are the Clifton Marine Baths.

4. *Clifton Marine Parade*, c. 1910, looking out to the River Thames with the West Street railway pier to the right. A new electricity pole has been erected in the foreground. This view shows the wharves with mounds of chalk ballast. Fletcher's wharf sent lime to London for use in the gasworks. The site was cleared to become the Imperial Paper Mills until the early 1980's, when again it was cleared to now become a shopping and industrial estate. Behind this was the rope walk of J. Knee and Son, who manufactured 'Rope, Line and Twine'. They also dealt in canvas, coir fenders, oil, oakum and many other similar products.

5. *The Clifton Marine Baths* were built in 1837 in this unique oriental style and offered hot and cold sea bathing. The original baths, dating from the 1790's, had sea bathing machines which were brought from Margate in 1796. These were wheeled out to allow bathers to test the 'medicinal quality' of the cold water and mud of the River Thames. As many as nine were in use at one time.

23148 Gravesend. The Yacht Club.

6. *The Royal Thames Yacht Club*, built in the 1790's by Mr. T. Pallister of the Falcon Inn as the Clifton Hotel. About 1863, it was acquired by the Union Yacht Club, which in turn was absorbed into the New Thames Yacht Club in 1869. The yacht club was a popular venue for Thames sailing races and was frequented by the Prince of Wales (King Edward VII). The first event of the yachting season was known as 'The Thames Sailing Week'. One of the most famous of the yachts to be seen off Gravesend, was the 'America', after which the America Cup is named. This was prior to being rebuilt in Northfleet, when it was known as the 'Camilla'. The yacht club became a V.A.D. hospital in the First World War, suffering a direct hit by bombs dropped from a Zeppelin, in 1915.

7. *The Baltic wharf in 1900*, with the West Street railway bridge and pier. The wharf handled timber from the Baltic Sea ports and was run by Mr. G. Willis. Both the wharf and the covered shed are full of stacked timber. This wharf passed on to Messrs. Tuffee and Hayward, coal and coke merchants, who operated the adjoining coal consumers wharf. On the railway pier can be seen a single railway carriage. The old yacht club on the right has a flag flying from the pole opposite.

THE PAPER MILLS. GRAVESEND

8. *The Imperial Paper Mills* c. 1910, looking down from the Overcliffe near Stuart Road, occupying the old chalk pits, the site of Clifton Marine Parade and associated buildings. The raised West Street railway line cuts across the site. In the distance are stacks of paper.

9. *Russell's Brewery*, in a view taken from the end of West Street railway pier c. 1910, showing the extensive buildings. Much of the old site is now converted into flats and offices. They produced the famous Shrimp Brand beer. George Wood and Sons Brewery was one of many small breweries taken over by Rusell's. In West Street on the old brewery wall, there is still a terracotta panel of the shrimp trademark. Truman, Hanbury, Buxton and Co. Ltd. eventually took over Russell's Brewery in 1931.

10. *The Terminus Hotel*, c. 1916. The Terminus was demolished and part of the Maltings housing complex is built on the site. Behind can be seen the end of the London, Chatham and Dover railway pier; an all-tides pier, which allowed the Batavier line to sail regularly to Rotterdam in Holland between the wars. Earlier, the Zeeland line used to sail to and from Flushing in Holland. The pier was also used by the paddle steamers, including the Golden Eagle, for pleasure trips.

11. *The Walton Belle paddle steamer,* 1899, had been launched by William Denny & Brothers, Dumbarton, only two years earlier. This view was taken off the West Street pier and shows the Walton Belle in the summer season with its decks full of passengers. Most of the paddle steamer operators openly flouted the permitted passenger numbers. The popular Walton Belle survived after being sold to New Medway Steam Packet Company, where she was renamed Essex Queen. She ended her days at Torquay as the Pride of Devon, where she was involved in a fatal collision. Due to her age and condition, she failed to gain a passengers' certificate and in 1951 was towed to the Thames to be scrapped at Grays in Essex. She was the last of the Belle paddle steamers.

12. *A view in 1900, of the River Thames*, with two young men admiring the scene. The smoke from the ship sailing downriver, curls up into the sky. Behind it are the sails of a three-masted sailing ship. Another large three-masted schooner is moored out in the river. The bow of the Tilbury Ferry is on the right.

Gravesend. Town Pier and Ferry.

13 *The Town Pier* was opened by the Earl of Darnley in July 1834. The construction was marred by the watermen, who believed their livelihood was threatened. The ensuing riot, which involved partial destruction of this temporary pier, required the attention of the yeomanry to quell it. The existing iron pier was constructed in 1836 and was covered over in 1854. The T-shaped pier projects 127 feet out into the River Thames, with an end measuring 76 by 30 feet. The pier was constructed with a pontoon, allowing passengers to alight at all times. It was a popular place for visitors admiring the view and at one time there was even a small band playing on the pier.

S 5833.   TOWN PIER AND FERRY, GRAVESEND

14. *The pontoon of the Town Pier* with the Tilbury and the Carlotta alongide. Passengers are alighting from the ferry and have to walk up the gangway and steps up to the pier. The Carlotta, built in 1892, was the first of the then-modern vessels. The Tilbury was built in 1883 and was used to take the Lord Mayor of London to open the new Tilbury Docks in 1886. The Carlotta was sold to the Essex Yacht Club and renamed the Gypsy, after being refitted as their 'clubhouse'.

THE FORESHORE & OLD GRAVESEND .

K.3047

15. *Looking along from the Town Pier* in this view of 1905, shows the many steps and small jetties in the river. The first steps led up to the Old Falcon and the next seps are those of the Old Amsterdam in East Street. George Wood's Brewery has a jetty with barrels stacked on it. St. Andrew's Waterside Mission can be seen behind. This church was erected in a north-south axis because of the narrow site, in 1870. The need for the mission was realised by Canon Robinson of Holy Trinity Church, to serve the emigrant ships, waiting off Gravesend. Amongst the donors towards the £1,000 building costs, was Charles Dickens. In the distance are Bawley Bay, the Clarendon Lawn and the covered slipway.

16. *Bawley Bay*, c. 1910, with seven shrimp boats. Bawley Bay was known as the Blockhouse Dock, associated with King Henry VIII's block house opposite the Clarendon. The shrimps of Gravesend were famous and used as the trademark of Russell's Brewery. The shrimping fleet declined and by the 1930's, only a few were left. The Thames estuary had long provided a rich fishing ground for the shrimps, which were boiled on board.

17. *The Clarendon Royal Hotel*, c. 1910. The view leads us along to the narrow East Street and the Clarendon shades in the distance. The Clarendon was originally the ordnance storekeeper's house and was opened as a hotel in about 1845. The name arises from the house being built for James II (then Duke of York and High Admiral), who married Anne, daughter of the Earl of Clarendon. Used by the upper classes, it had as a guest, in 1863, the Prince of Wales (later King Edard VII).

Grounds of Clarendon Royal Hotel, Gravesend. 16.

18. *The Clarendon lawn*, a former bowling green, was said to be the most famous in Gravesend, with a surface like a billiard table. The lawns were ruined when dances were held on them. Part of the lawn was used for playing tennis. During the First World War a pontoon bridge was set up from the lawn across the Thames to Essex, using 70 barges. The 'bridge' was struck by shipping several times. Alongside the lawn are the remains of the old block house of King Henry VIII.

ROYAL TERRACE PIER, GRAVESEND.

No. 5046

19. *Sailing barge*, c. 1906. The sailing barge is moored at West's barge builders, which started around 1904 and included a covered slipway. West's used their barges to carry goods across the Channel during the First World War and also were amongst the first to fit motors to their barges. Near the barge works, occupying the site of Milton wharf, was the London Lead Oxide Works. Prior to this, the site was a fodder business and a sweet factory. The original site was the Terrace Gardens and the works were built on the site of one of the old open bandstands.

S 16921   Terrace Pier, Gravesend

20. *The Terrace Pier* was originally erected opposite the Clarendon in 1832. The current pier, in line with Harmer Street, was built in 1842 and was quite unique in respect of being the first to have cast-iron cylinders as its foundation. The pier was surrounded by the Terrace Pier Gardens with their attractions. In 1892, the unsafe state of the pier endangered the users and it was bought by the Trinity House Pilots from the Receiver of the Court of Chancery.

The Frozen Thames at Gravesend, 1895

21. *The frozen Thames* in the Great Frost of 1895. This was reminiscent of the early frosts in London, caused by the narrow bridges restricting the flow. The bawley boats are trapped by the huge ice flows. Much of the river traffic was prevented from working.

34699. Gravesend Pier. C.N.

22. *Royal Terrace Pier* in 1905, with 12 sailing barges and several tugs in view. On the eastern side of the pier was the Anglo-American wharf, established there in 1924. The wharf and adjoining oil depot serviced a large area. Fuel pumps supplied motor vessels in the Thames.

23. *The Sea School* was originally the Sailors' Home from 1886 until 1918, when the Sea School occupied the building. The Sea School was required to train sailors for the merchant navy, following the terrible losses of the First World War. The Triton, an old paddle schooner launched in 1882, was given to the school in 1919 and was moored off the jetty. The first captain superintendent was Captain Oswald Lewis, in charge of a potential of 300 boys. The new Sea School was built in 1967 on the marshes at Denton. The old Sea School has since been demolished. The old rotunda watch tower of the customs house is in the foreground.

24. *The customs house* in a drawing by Llwyd Roberts. This elegant building was erected in 1816, for the excise department, with the customs sharing the building in 1819. The site was originally the Fountain Inn, which was moved across the road.

99550 The Promenade. Gravesend

25. *The promenade* on a hot summer's day in the mid-1920's The shelters providing a shaded relief were erected in 1906. The 'beach', without groynes, appears mud-free, in contrast with the view in 1993. The promenade was a salt marsh and was leased from the War Office in 1886, at a cost of £10 per annum. G.M. Arnold, eight times mayor of Gravesend, gave a further area to the town in 1890. The bandstand was erected in 1890 at a cost of £100. The early promenade had a wall, built partly of cement, salvaged when a schooner, the Spring, was wrecked. These cement bags were visible until quite recently, when the new river defences were built.

26. *Fort House*, General Gordon's house from 1865 to 1871, was one of several, moved on rollers from the eastern side of the 13th-century Milton chantry. This view shows the front of the house in 1907 in Milton Place with an almost country cottage appearance.

Fort House, Gravesend.   74.

27. *Fort House*, a rear view, showing the timber construction. The house was at one time a school and the town clerk's house. General Gordon carried his charitable work among the poor boys of the town, educating and feeding them. The house and several other buildings in Milton Place were destroyed by a V2 in 1944.

28. *The memorial service for King Edward VII* in 1910, on the promenade and recreation ground, with the mayor and council on the raised platform. Hundreds of people and a choir are in attendance. Around 1911, further improvements were made to the promenade and a swimming pool was erected on this site with water heated from the power station (chimney visible in the distance).

Will Driscolls Royal Sparks, Gravesend. 1914.   2.

29. *The Alfresco Theatre* on the promenade with Will Driscoll's Royal Sparks. Promenade concerts were always a popular attraction. The programme in 1910 for L. Austin's Concerts advertised the following: 'These popular concerts take place daily at 3 and 7.30. A company of talented, refined artistes in an up-to-date programme. Acknowledge by all to be one of the finest and best Alfresco Entertainments ever seen in Gravesend. Sacred concerts every Sunday evening at 8.30. Chairs 3d, 2d and 1 d.'

Statue General Gordon, in Gordon's Gardens, Gravesend

30. *The statue of General Gordon*, made by Doulton & Co. in buff-coloured terra-cotta, was unveiled by the mayor, G.M. Arnold, in 1893. The statue is of General Gordon in Royal Engineers uniform, with his sword at his side and a cane in his hand. The cane was referred to by the Chinese soldiers of his 'ever victorious army' as 'Gordon's wand of victory'. The General Gordon Memorial Gardens were presented to Gravesend by G.M. Arnold.

Gravesend. Entrance to Gordon Grounds

31. *The entrance to the Gordon Grounds*, with the cast-iron drinking fountain and the stone obelisk inside the gardens. This has a commemorative plate regarding the donation of the ground by G.M. Arnold. The stone was moved in 1892 from the canal, where it had replaced the 'Round Tree' which had previously marked the Port of London's seaward limit. Following damage from use as a target, arson and finally storm, the obelisk was erected in the tree's place. The pathway behind the fountain is now known as Khartoum Walk, in memory of General Gordon.

32. *The canal lock* c. 1906, with a sailing barge about to enter. The canal was conceived in 1799, by Ralph Dodd, with military intentions: to save the mileage and time between the Thames and the Medway. Construction was estimated at two years, and was started soon afterwards, but was finally completed in 1824. One of the products shipped along the canal, was horse manure from London for use on farms as fertiliser. The end of the canal basin became the terminus for the Gravesend and Rochester Railway, opening for service in 1845. It was acquired the following year by the South Eastern Railway. In 1913, the Gravesend Sailing Club built a club house on land, bought from the South Eastern and Chatham Railway, adjacent to the canal lock. The canal basin is now separated from the remains of the canal by an industrial estate.

33. *The old boathouse* in 1906, with the wide canal and open marshes to the rear. The boathouse was made of an upturned boat and was said to be the idea for Charles Dicken's 'Peggoty's Boat House'. The old boathouse was the home of a boatowner who rented out pleasure boats on the canal for the visitors.

THE CANAL, GRAVESEND.　　　No. 5004

34. *A swing bridge on the canal.* This was one of several on the canal. The canal had a steam tug, used to help the barges along. The canal was not a success and the tunnel section at Higham was used for the track bed of the new railway. Despite a proposal for a new canal in 1902, the last traffic was only able to use the canal to as far as Higham.

35. *The Ship and Lobster*, c. 1906, with a group of soldiers 'marching' to the Denton ranges. Their appearance, however, indicates a visit to the nearby pub, the Ship and Lobster. The inn had a tea garden, skittle alley and swings, to attract the visitor. It was also used to hold inquests on bodies recovered from the River Thames. A proposal to build a mortuary next door never materialised. The path along which the soldiers are 'marching', led further on to Shorne Mead Fort. For a considerable time after the First World War this popular path was closed to the public.

36. *The range wardens and markers at Milton ranges*, c. 1905, with lowered target. The ranges were used by soldiers from Milton barracks, Gravesend, as well as the Royal Marines and sailors from Chatham. Great care was taken to avoid stray shots. Around this time the commanding officer was from the Royal Marines. These ranges also had their own railway halt.

37. *This view of Denton* shows the Prince of Wales public house, previously a farmhouse, in the distance at the junction with Elliott Street. At one time the Prince of Wales had a tea garden and bowling green in addition to a well-stocked cellar of wine. The bowling green was used by the oldest bowls club in the district, The Gravesend and Milton. The shop next door was a grocer's and also a Post Office. On the opposite corner, the former bakery became the Co-operative Society – grocers and butchers. The row of houses continues until the long, red and white striped barber's pole of the hairdresser's can be seen. The tram lines are just visible and lead to the terminus near to where the picture was taken. Denton, a tiny parish of 435 acres, was almost entirely owned by G.M. Arnold and Lewis Raphael.

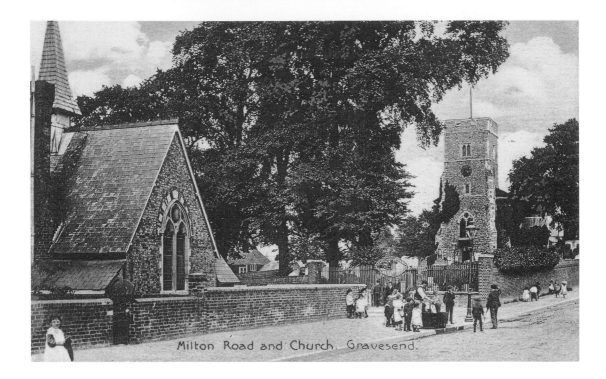

Milton Road and Church, Gravesend.

38. *The Church School* was built in 1861, with extensions being added in 1886. The school had the name 'Duck Pond School' as a result of the pond nearby. The school was part of the 'National Schools' scheme and remained in use until just before the Second World War. It continued to serve the community as the parish hall. The old school/parish hall needed expensive repairs and was sold to help fund the new church centre, erected on the north side of Milton church. The churchyard wall in the distance has ornate iron railings and gate where the present lychgate stands.

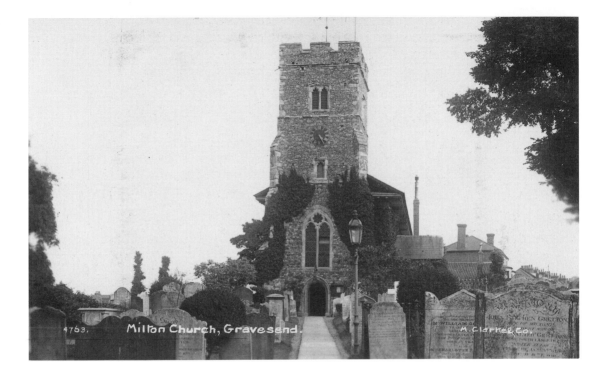

Milton Church, Gravesend.

39. *The church at Milton next Gravesend*, dedicated to St. Peter and St. Paul, is of 14th-century construction. A church is mentioned in the 'Textus Roffensis' of 975 and the Domesday Book in 1087, although no trace of this earlier church exists. The roof of the church is its most unusual feature. In 1700, following the theft of lead, it was found that the existing roof needed attention. The result was the removal of the old crenelations and roof. The replacement roof gives it an oriental appearance.

40. *This view shows* two of the original and the two newly presented bells of Milton Church, about to be rehung. The bells were dedicated by the Dean of Rochester on 23rd October 1930. The large bell to the left was cast in 1930 by Mears and Stainbank Founders London, 'given in Memory of Alan Gates Sandford killed at Loos 1915 and F.W. Mitchell 21 years leader'. The centre bell on the hook and chain is the largest (42'). It is marked: 'John Hodson made mee 1656. MASARS I.S.T.M. and P.B. William Antrobus, John Hall, Church-wardens.' The right-hand bell is marked: 'M and S London given by Churchwardens Ernest E. and Mrs. L.E. Knowles 1930. G.W. Mennie M.A. 30 years Rector.' The bells were raised by a hand-operated steel cable winch on the left. The fourth bell is behind the winch.

41. *The sundial* in this view of 1900 is on the south porch of Milton church. The sundial was the work of James Giles, master of the Free School, and bears the legend 'Trifle not, your time's but short'. Pocock, in his 'History of Gravesend', 1797, devotes nearly a page to the workings of the sundial. The porch was used as a vestry and is now a small chapel. The last incumbent, Reverend Hilary Day, restored the sundial.

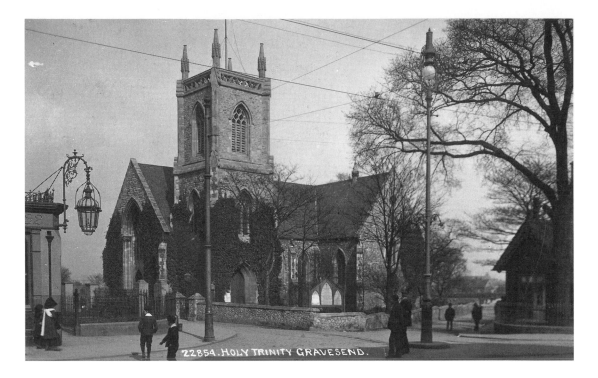

42. *Holy Trinity Church* was erected in 1844 on a site donated by the War Department. The church was built of soft Kent ragstone, with a slate roof, and had a capacity of about 1,000. There was also a small school alongside, built in 1866, for 250 pupils. The new school with the same name was built in Milton barracks. The church served the community of this part of the town for over 100 years, until population shift to residential areas being built to the south, reduced the congregation. The church was demolished in 1963. The site is now the British Telecommunications car park and is surrounded by a high wire fence. The ornate lamp on the left is from the Globe public house. On the right can be seen the small thatched cottage that stood where the present telephone exchange now is.

43. *Milton Road* is seen in this early view, showing the shop of Cunningham's Opticians on the right, at No. 18. There was no mistaking their premises with an enormous pair of spectacles on the parapet. They advertised as 'specialists in sight testing, spectacles, repairs and matchings'. This photograph, taken in the summer of 1906, shows the spire of the newly-erected Methodist Church behind the clock tower. The British Tar public house is on the right, at the end of the shop blinds.

Modern School, Gravesend.

Photo. C. E. Dixon.

44. *The Modern School (Middle Class School)* in Peacock Street was run by a Mr. C. Hooper-Smith, who advertised the following: 'a thoroughly sound and practical Education is guaranteed, subjects of study being chosen with a view to each boy's capabilities and intended career.' Special classes were available for short-hand, callisthenics and violin. The school was subsequently run by a Mr. Waldgrave. The building became a dancing school, known as Freeborn's Hall. It was also home for Lewis's Printers and at present is a Sikh 'cash and carry' store.

The Clock Tower, Gravesend.

45. *The clock tower* was erected as the 'Jubilee Clock Tower' to commemorate Queen Victoria's golden jubilee. The building costs were raised by public subscription. The foundation stone was laid by the mayor, William Fletcher, on 6th September 1887. Lord Grimthorpe was instrumental in the design of the clock which was based on Big Ben. The chimes were donated in 1890 by Alfred Tolhurst and were possibly those from the old Rosherville clock tower. The brick-built tower was faced in Portland stone with bands of Dumfries stone. It originally had four gas lanterns at the base.

46. *The Harmer House School* in the tree-lined, fashionable Grove, was run by a Mr. W.H. Hedger A.K.C. It was one of about six such schools in Gravesend for 'the younger gentlemen'. My wife's great-grandfather, the first Lewis Solomon, was a pupil there in the 1860's. Nearly fifty pupils, wearing mortar boards as part of their uniform, are visible in this view, taken in the 1880's. Harmer House became the laundry for Shaw and Sons. The building has now been demolished.

47. *Harmer Street and the Grand Theatre* are in this view of about 1900. Harmer Street was built in 1836 as part of an elaborate and grand scheme by the Milton Park Estate, whose Chairman was Alderman Harmer. The concept was for Harmer Street to open out in a circle, where now only Berkley Crescent is, and then along what is now the Grove (then Upper Harmer Street) to the foot of Windmill Hill. The Grand Theatre with its four huge columns, was a popular concert venue. It was built as the Literary Institute and changed names several times. The site is now remembered by the Call Boy public house. In the centre of the picture one of the booths is visible, situated at the entrance to the old Terrace Pier Gardens.

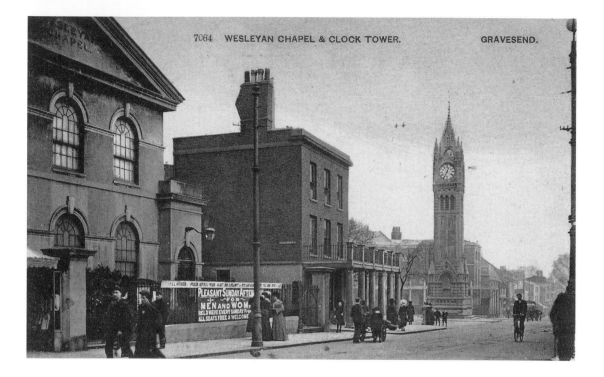

48. *The Wesleyan Methodist Church*, Milton Road, was built in 1812 as the Ebeneezer Chapel. The increasing congregation required the building to be enlarged and this was carried out in 1841, when the frontage, seen in the view, was added. The Church Sunday School was held in Peacock Street and the sign in front of the church proclaims, 'Pleasant Sunday Afternoons For Men and Women'. The space behind the railings at the front of the church provided a small burial ground.

49. *The new Wesleyan Church* with the sign of the railing announcing 'Church Opening', in June 1906. The church was built in the decorated gothic style of red brick and Bath stone, at a cost of over £10,000. The builder was Mr. A.E. Tong and the architects were Morley & Sons. The church was built for 800 and had a school behind it, which was completed and opened earlier.

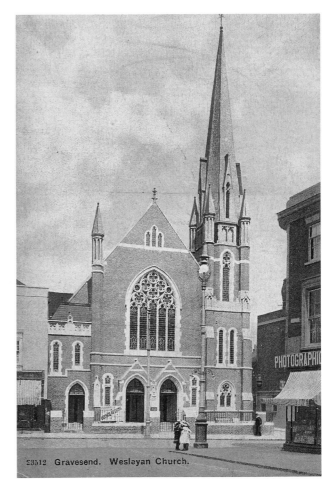

23512 Gravesend. Wesleyan Church.

Milton Road & King Street, Gravesend.

50. *Milton Road* in this view of about 1910, shows the shop of Clarke and Co. Clarke's produced postcards of Gravesend and District along with the 'Cheapest Printing in Gravesend'. The shop front is full of their wares. Miss Rawlinsons' shop at Nos 4 and 5, sold baby-linen. This picture also shows the early form of electric street lighting in Gravesend. The tram lines, set in cobble stones, lead past the New Inn and Mitre Inn at the corner of Queen Street.

51. *This view of the New Inn, Milton Road*, taken about 1913, shows the inn with beautifully decorated advertising signs for Rigden's Fine Ales. Behind the inn are Turner's livery stables, who offered char-à-banc drives daily. The New Inn was once the family home of Dr. Holker, who accommodated the Prince and Princess of Orange in 1734. They sheltered there, due to unfavourable sailing weather. It was sold in the 1780's, to become the New Inn, named as such, perhaps, because the licensee was from the New Tavern. The New Inn, a former coaching inn, boasted a large garden at the rear, with a bowling green.

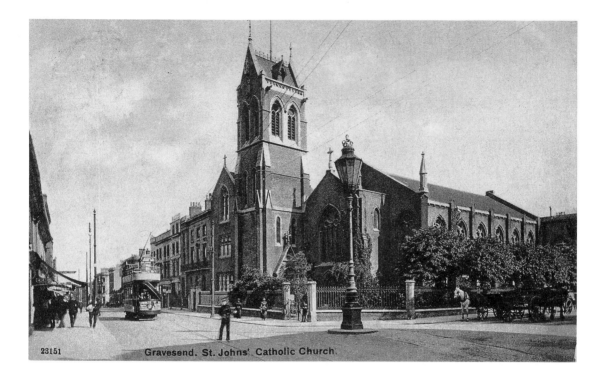

23151 Gravesend. St. Johns' Catholic Church.

52. *St. John's Roman Catholic Church* was built in 1834 as a chapel of ease and sold to the Catholic Church by Reverend W.J. Blew in 1851. The tower was built in 1873. Railings and shrubs surround the front of the church. Alongside, in Parrock Street, was a standing for the char-à-bancs. The magnificent lamp in the centre of the picture stands at least 25 feet high and is surmounted by a crown.

GRAVESEND FROM AN AEROPLANE. PARROCK STREET. ROYAL TERRACE PIER. THAMES MISSION CHURCH. (A4018)

53. *This aerial view of* Parrock Street and adjoining roads shows St. Andrew's Mission at the top. Moving down Queen Street, many houses can be seen that were once in East Street, Crooked Lane, the Terrace and Terrace Street. The area around Parrock Street, bottom left of the view, was also cleared away. This has provided Gravesend, for over twenty years, with a vast car park, now overlooked by two large blocks of flats.

King Street, Gravesend. No. 1984.

54. *King Street* in about 1915, with a policeman standing in the centre of the view. The premises of Bryant and Rackstraws are on the left. They took over the business of Caddell's Printers adjoining, and offered a comprehensive service to Gravesend as drapers, furnishers, etc. including a lending library and book service. The present Westminster Bank on the right, was built on the site of the old almshouses in 1898. The Daimler omnibus alongside David Greig's, built in 1903, was operated by the North Kent Motor Services. It was part of the Gravesend and Northfleet Electric Tramway Co. from 1913 to 1920, when the service was taken over by Maidstone and District.

55. *This view of New Road* shows the Nelson Hotel, landlord Thomas Hooper, with the hotel part in the foreground. The centre lower section was the billiards room and the western end the Nelson shades. The former Nelson used to be a coaching inn and stables, jutting out into the New Road. The vacant lot for sale beyond the Nelson was Steel's stonemason's yard. It is now the site of the Midland Bank. The Prince of Orange, commercial inn, has a large notice offering luncheon daily, from 12.30 to 2.30. This was also in its time another coaching inn and was demolished in the 1920's, to become Burton's. The adjoining 'Wonderful Mutoscope', with the enticing 'Admission Free', was an amusement arcade with 'what the butler saw machines'. Trees are visible on the south side of New Road.

23507 Gravesend. High Street.

56. *This view of the High Street* shows the town hall with its attractive columned front, which was added in 1836. On the top of the town hall were three huge statues of 'Justice, Truth and Minerva'. (These were removed for safety before the last war, but what happened to them, I have been unable to establish.) The original boundary between Gravesend and Milton Parish ran down the centre of the High Street. Its narrowness caused many problems for horse-drawn wagons and pedestrians. Many hanging and other shop advertising signs can be seen, along with some very ornate lamps. Jury Street leads off to the left.

57. *This postcard shows the view of High Street* from Town Pier Square. The narrow road on the right is West Street before 'The Kent and Essex, Ironmongery and Ship Chandlery Stores' was demolished to widen the road. The High Street is full of busy shops, public houses and restaurants. A row of about ten timber weatherboard houses is on the right, with numerous advertising signs projecting into the High Street.

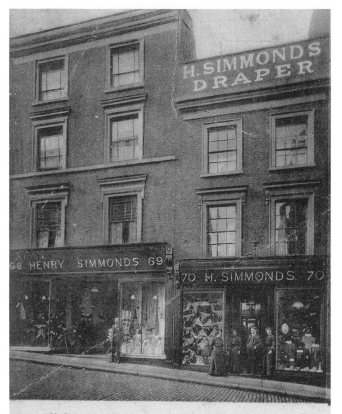

H. SIMMONDS, 68, - 69, - 70, High St., Gravesend.
Noted House for Good Value. Established over 100 Years.

58. *This advertising card* of Henry Simmonds of 68, 69 and 70 High Street, Gravesend, shows the sales assistants, standing in the doorways of the shop. Simmonds were established around 1800. The shop advertised as 'Undertaker, Dress and Mantle Maker and Milliner'. The High Street was always a bustling and busy shopping area, serving not only the townsfolk and nearby inhabitants, but also the many visitors to Gravesend. The High Street since has suffered, not only with the loss of the housing on either side, but also because of a shift westwards of the main shopping area. The result is, that today the lower end of the High Street is a scene of desolation.

59. *St. George's Church* in this view is shown surrounded by buildings. The smoking chimney in the distance is of Russell's Brewery and the end of the West Street railway pier can be seen. Just below the chimney is the Church Street School, built in 1876 to accommodate over 480 pupils, including infants. Much of the area was cleared in the early 1960's, leaving eventually only the church. Also in the view is a three-masted sailing ship on the River Thames. The Tilbury Hotel, built in 1886, is visible behind. This hotel was constructed mainly of timber on over 400 piles. In 1944 it was bombed and destroyed by fire.

St. George's Parish Church of Gravesend (Exterior).

60. *St. George's Church* was built in 1731, on the site of the previous church, which was destroyed in a fire in 1727. The church, designed by Charles Sloane, was built of local brick and dressed in Bath stone. The church had had additions: the chancel in 1892 and the north aisle in 1897. The church closed in 1952, reopening when Holy Trinity Church closed in 1962. Following the demolition of St. James' Church in 1968, it resumed a rightful position as the parish church of Gravesend. The church is noted, particularly in the U.S.A., as the burial place of the Indian Princess Pocahontas. Her statue stands in the churchyard and, according to the register, she was buried as Rebecca Wrolfe in the chancel of the earlier church, in 1616.

61. *Windmill Street* showing the recently opened public library on the right. Built of stone and red brick, it was opened in 1905 by G.M. Arnold, the mayor. Andrew Carnegie offered the finance, provided a suitable site could be obtained. The site was purchased for the sum of 1,000 guineas, funded by various prominent towns-folk and businesses. Andrew Carnegie was given the freedom of the borough as a result. A pawnbroker's sign can be seen on the left. This sign, minus the balls, is still there. In the distance is Bryant and Rackstraw's shop. The tram lines ran down both sides of the road.

23505 Gravesend. Windmill Street and Public Library.

62. *Windmill Street,* with railings on the left surrounding the old burial ground. This was used from 1788, as an extension for St. George's churchyard, until 1854, when the last interment was carried out. The burial ground became rubbish strewn and in 1888 was acquired by the council and turned into Woodville Gardens. The tram is travelling from the terminus at the old Prince of Orange, into the town. Most of the houses still have their front gardens, complete with cast-iron railings. Harry Legg's carriers premises are on the right.

63. *The beautiful rear garden of the Station Hotel*, where the regulars are enjoying their pints of beer. Behind them can be seen the allotments where the Rathmore Road car park was built in the late 1950's. Before the houses were built on the left-hand side, the route was known as Blackberry Lane. In the distance, at the end of the allotments, is Hutchinson Place, built in the early 1830's and named after the owner of the land.

S 5822

CENTRAL STATION, GRAVESEND.

64. *The railway station was opened in 1849*, the architect being Samuel Beazley. The London-bound side was the more impressive with its tall columns. The station had a turntable, water tower and goods sidings. This view, looking west, shows the platform and canopies, with the iron footbridge over the line. The old Darnley Road bridge can be seen in the distance. The station was much used in the early days by royalty, arriving and departing from the Royal Terrace Pier.

65. *New Road* in 1905, with the Colonial Meat Company on the left, advertising New Zealand mutton and American beef. The import of meat from America, Australia and New Zealand was made possible by the new, refrigerated ships. The 'Oil, Color and Varnish Stores' are on the right with various products advertised on its wall. The solitary tram is making its way along New Road to the terminus at Denton.

NEW ROAD, GRAVESEND

66. *This view of New Road*, posted in 1916, but taken a few years earlier at the height of summer, shows two soldiers in a cart, riding along the tram tracks. Missing's Bazaar is decorated with St. Georges and Union Flags. On the right, just past E. Mason, saddlers, can be seen the scaffolding poles of the new Midland Bank.

67. *New Road at the junction with Garrick Street* shows the Salvation Army hall, purchased in 1883, on the right. The hall was built as the Theatre Royal in 1807, by a Mr. J. Trotter. The stables in Royal Mews, next door, were once the livery stables of Lewis Solomon. As carriage master, he provided char-à-banc and other services, in addition to his main business as funeral furnishers. The next building was the Eagle tavern. This whole corner is now occupied by Tesco's. The row of shopblinds on the left continues in an almost unbroken line along the road.

S 5827   LONDON ROAD, GRAVESEND.

68. *The Public Halls and Restaurant* is the large building on the right. The halls date from around 1880 and are shown in this view being used as a U.S.A. roller skating rink, a craze at the turn of the century. The halls were used as a cinema from 1912, the earliest in Gravesend. The char-à-banc outside the hall is one owned by Solomon's, who advertised a 'Trip to Cobham, 1/- return, from the Public Halls'. The bakery at the corner of Bath Street is still there today and also the sign on the tram pole outside, indicating to the hospital. In the distance is the Invicta Cycle Works, next to St. James' School.

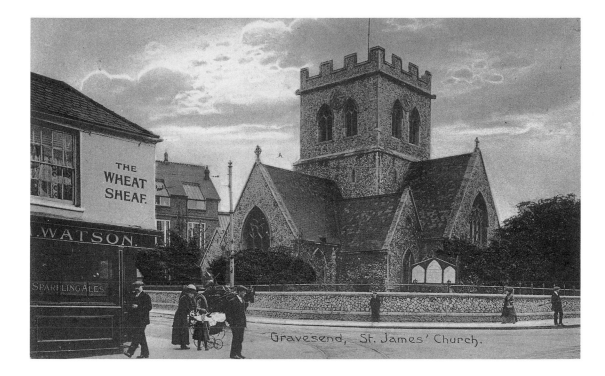

Gravesend, St. James' Church.

69. *The Wheatsheaf public house* on the corner of Darnley Road is shown in its original clapboarded state. St. James' Church was built in 1852 and demolished in 1968. The first incumbent, Reverend John Joynes, is remembered by the name of the K.C.C. offices on the site, 'Joynes House'. Only a few original houses are left in New Road and around the corner in Darnley Road, mainly visible by their roof structures and timber clapboarding at the rear.

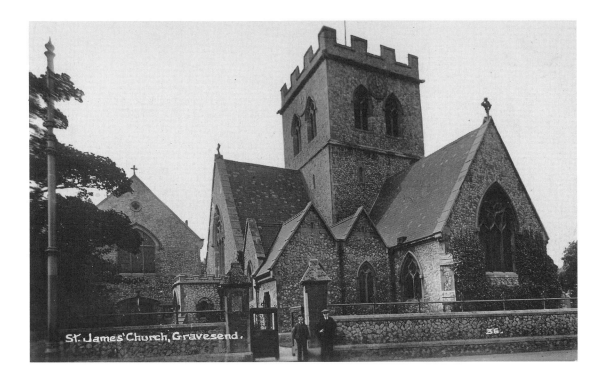

70. *St. James' Church* was built in 1851 of Kent ragstone. Seating was originally provided for 827. The first minister was Reverend Joyn Joynes (1851-1883). The vicarage, behind the church in the Overcliffe, was presented by Reverend E. Mort. The old church was demolished in 1968, after acting as the parish church for Gravesend from 1952. The old oak altar was given to the Cobham parish Church.

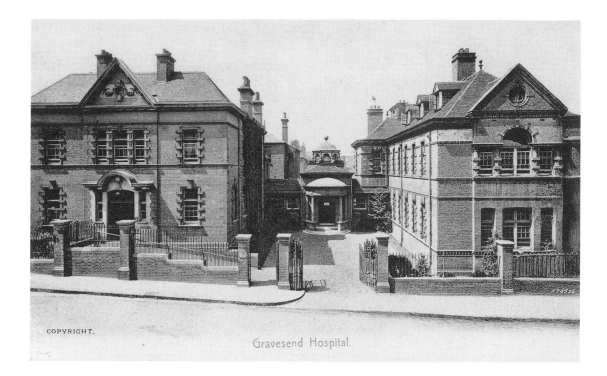

Gravesend Hospital.

71. *Gravesend Hospital* in Bath Street had its origins in a small dispensary, which had been established in 1850 in Milton Road, at the corner of Wellington Street. Several local business people and Lord Darnley helped fund this charitable venture. The need for a hospital was apparent and land donated by Lord Darnley in Bath Street realised this gaol. In 1854, the new dispensary and infirmary were opened, the architect being John Gould. This was the start of the hospital, which by the 1880's was known as the Gravesend Hospital and was run by voluntary contribution.

GRAVESEND HOSPITAL.

72. *This view of the interior* of a female ward in Gravesend Hospital, shows the neatly made beds with every-one, including patients, posed for the photograph. The ward is lit by gas, as shown by the hanging lamp. None of the windows have curtains and there is no evidence of any form of screening, for privacy. The only greenery is provided on the table in the foreground, covered with flower vases and potted palms.

1990 Gravesend. Technical School.

73. *The foundation stone of the Technical School* was laid in 1892, and the building was opened by Their Royal Highnesses, Princess Beatrice and Prince Henry of Battenberg on 19th July 1893. The Technical School was designed by Lt. Col. Plunkett C.B.E. A new wing was added and opened in 1901, to accommodate a central hall, laboratories and workshop. The statue of Queen Victoria, in front, was presented by G.M. Arnold, to commemorate her diamond jubilee in 1897.

S 16923 Darnley Road, Gravesend

74. *Darnley Road*, described as 'another charming spot: the houses here are mostly semi-detached, standing in gardens sweetly decked in floral beauty, opening out upon a fine outspread country'. It was at one time a favourable part of the town, and the 'well-to-do' business people lived there. This country road had a high bank on the west side and was considered preferable to Pelham Road, which suffered with the tram system. The northern section was once known as Somerset Street.

75. *Elephants from 'Lord' John Sanger's Circus* can be seen in this view, leaving Darnley Road and entering Arthur Street. The circus, a regular visitor to Gravesend, was encamped on the area behind the Overcliffe and Lennox Road, before St. James' Avenue was built. The procession, with crowds of people watching, consists of four elephants, three camels, followed by a horse and wagon. The circus was originally owned by 'Lord' George Sanger and his brother John. 'Lord' George Sanger, the founder of the showman's guild, was murdered in 1911.

76. *The quadrangle of the County School for Girls* in Pelham Road. The school was opened on 20th October
1926, by the Duchess of Atholl. The site used to be a cow pasture and was also used as a sports field, users
including Gravesend United Football Club. The school became the Girls' Grammar School in 1944.

GRAVESEND. 61362.

77. *This view towards Gravesend was taken around 1910*, from the top of the Rosherville clock tower. The view over the fields, where Marina Drive now is, shows the small stationmasters' house at Rosherville. The spire of Rosherville church is centre left, with an almost deserted road leading to Gravesend. Lennox Road, with only a few houses, cuts across the middle and in the distance are the tall trees that line Pelham Road.

78. *Pelham Road and Old Road West* are seen in this view of 1910, with the small triangle in the centre of the junction. The shopping parade contains the depot for Shaw's Laundry. The tram lines in the foreground, come from the depot at the Bridge Inn in Dover Road and lead on, up Pelham Road, towards the town. Pelham Road was formerly known as Manor Lane and Styles Lane, before the housing developments of the late-Victorian age.

79. *This is the opposite view* to the previous one and is looking towards Dover Road and Northfleet. The shop blinds are almost all out. On the left, out of the picture, are the Pelham Arms and the Post Office of Richard Haill, who was also an undertaker. The only traffic is provided by the horse-drawn carts, coming out of Pelham Road South.

80. *Pelham Road South* leads on to Perry Street, Northfleet. There is a handcart being pushed down the centre of the road. This whole area was church or 'glebe' land, remembered by Glebe Road, on the right, in Pelham Road South. The hoarding with its posters on the left, advertises: 'Camp Coffee, Turog Bread, Robin Starch and The grand opening of The Pavilion Skating Rink.' The rink was opened in 1910, in Grange Road, off Pelham Road, as a result of the roller skating craze.

81. *Old Road West*, looking west with the cemetery entrance by the trees on the left. The builders' yard of Beal and Hubbard is on the right, followed by a long line of houses with the showrooms of Waters and Wilks, stonemasons, opposite the cemetery gates. The cemetery started out as the Victoria Gardens in 1834, and the present chapel building was used for dances and concerts. It failed because of the distance from the town and competition from the new Rosherville gardens. Most of the ground was sold, in 1839, to the Gravesend and Milton Cemetery Company.

THE ALMSHOUSES . GRAVESEND

82. *The almshouses in Old Road West* were built in 1897 on the site of Reed's Cottages, previously used to house cholera victims and the poor, Henry Pinnock, by his will of 1624, benefited the poor of Gravesend and Milton and the original almshouses. The Post Office can be seen on the opposite corner of Wrotham Road. This section of the almshouses had to be demolished owing to subsidence. They were recently replaced by a more modern development.

83. *The Service Garage, Wrotham Road*, is depicted here, with its petrol pump on the edge of the pavement. On the left is a warning sign for the nearby Wrotham Road School. Ornate B.P. lanterns are mounted on the top of the gates and the showroom windows are full of bicycles for sale. The Service garage was an A.A. and R.A.C. agent and the A.A. sign can be seen above the building. This and the adjoining shops were demolished to make way for the present petrol station.

"Wood Lands Park". "Gravesend."

84. *Woodlands Park* with the newly erected King George V memorial gates. The park celebrates its 60th anniversary in 1994 and is a former meadow. The children, then as now, are playing cricket and one boy can be seen doing handstands. Many of the large trees have since been felled and behind the dense group of trees is Woodlands, built in 1893, former home of George Wood of Wood's Brewery.

85. *Huggins' Cottages* at the corner of Cross Lane West and Wrotham Road. The charitable work of Mrs. Huggins, when her husband was mayor, realised the funds through 'Tipperary Fairs', to build these cottages for disabled servicemen. The land was donated by T.C. Colyer-Fergusson in memory of his son. The cottages were opened in 1922. The small trees have now grown tall and hide this view. The card was sent by Mrs. Huggins in 1923, regarding more charity work involving the NSPCC.

10586. OLD ROAD WEST, GRAVESEND.

86. *This view of Old Road West* shows the road near to where the present Elmfield Close is, in about 1905. The present doctor's and dentist's surgery, Elmfield, was the former home of W. Fletcher of Fletcher's wharf. The small monkey-puzzle tree on the left grew to a great height, only to suffer from the 'hurricane' of October 1987. The increasing housing developments of the late Victorian and early Edwardian era were gradually encroaching on this rural road, popular for country walks.

87. *The Old Prince of Orange Inn* in Old Road East was built in the 18th century as a coaching inn. The name was then the Prince of Orange, but the 'Old' was added when the New Road was cut in 1801. The New Prince of Orange stood at the top of the High Street. The inn was replaced in the early 1930's by the present 'Tudorbethan' building. At one time there was an archery ground and cricket pitch connected with the inn. The view shows the inn under the landlordship of W. W. Bardoe and a row of interesting advertising posters can be seen alongside. The tram terminus was in front.

88. *Singlewell Road* in the 1920's, with the off-licence of G.E. Tonge to the left. Next was Chapman's confectionery and tobacconist shop. At the corner 1 Cross Lane West was Hammond's bakery and sweet shop from 1884 until 1967. Hammond's Corner is still remembered to this day. On the right-hand side of the road were the nurseries of Frank Badman, who lived at No. 30. The shop on the opposite corner to the right, became Rothwell's Stores. 'Rothwell's the Reliable Grocers' also had grocery stores in Echo Square and Northfleet. Singlewell Road is almost deserted, apart from the lone cyclist and the odd pedestrian.

Echo Square. Gravesend.

40380

89. *Echo Square and Cross Lane East.* This view shows Bartholomew's Newsagents, with the advertising boards of the Daily Mail announcing: 'The Kaiser – another illness.' The shops were built on the site of Sun Cottage. The newly erected St. Faith's Hall (1907) and houses of Ferndale Road are just visible above the heads of the two girls standing in the dirt road. The Post Office was on the right and survived for over 80 years, finally closing in 1982.

90. *This view of Cross Lane East*, posted in 1930, contrasts with the view of Sun Cottage, taken from the same position over 20 years earlier. The parade brought shops to the new housing developments to the south of Gravesend. They were the Gravesend Co-operative Society Ltd. shops and a bakery. In the parade were also W.J. Hunt, builder and carpenter, Clark's confectioners and G.W. Mason's grocers.

91. *Old Sun Cottage* in Cross Lane, in about 1905, with the handcart of Mr. Hemming, the baker of 66 Granville road, in front. The cottage, a former beerhouse, with a backdrop of elm trees, was demolished around 1908. It had a small weatherboarded and thatched barn alongside. The end of the horsetrough in the centre of Echo Square, can just be seen on the left. The lane behind was also known as Old Sun Lane and Sun Pond Lane. The latter name came from the pond at the end of what is now Portland Avenue. It was said to be deep enough to have drowned a boy who fell in from an overhanging tree.

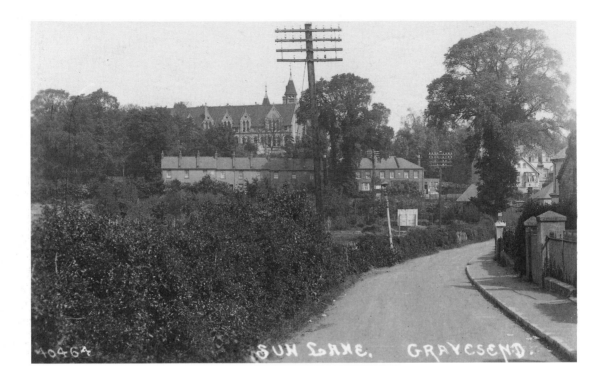

SUN LANE. GRAVESEND.

92. *Sun Lane*, in a rural aspect, was also home for Charles Hooper-Smith of the Middle Class School, who lived at 'Sunny Vale'. The picture shows Sun Lane as a dirt road with single footpath on the east side. The west side of the lane was not yet developed and an advertising board for land sales can be seen in the distance. The upper part of Milton Mount College and Elnathan Cottages in Cross Lane East are in the centre of the view.

93. *Parrock Road*, looking south towards Echo Square and Whitehill Road, with its neat hedgerows and gardens. A haystack from Parrock Farm is on the left in a field bordered by a chestnut fence. The gate faces Echo Square and the horsetrough. The land to the left now contains houses and a parade of shops in Echo Square.

94. *Parrock Road*, looking north, with the horsetrough in the centre of the road being used by a pony and trap. The red granite horsetrough and drinking fountain was erected in memory of Kendrick and Annie Martha Gibbons, in 1903. It is shown with an ornate lamp. The road was only single lane at this time and the rural aspect is enhanced by the tall trees and shrubs. On the left, hidden by these trees, is Milton Mount College.

SOUTHFLEET 4½
DARTFORD 7½

B DARTFORD 6½
26 LONDON 23½

ROCHESTER 7½ B
CANTERBURY 32½ 26½

Parrock Road, Gravesend.

99383.

95. *This view of Parrock Road* was taken about ten years later and is without the horsetrough, which had been moved to the west side of Echo Square. There it remained until a few years ago, when it was placed to the centre of Echo Square. The triangle in the centre of Echo Square, with the new road direction signs and benches, shows what was possible in the 1920's, without the traffic of today. The trees of the earlier view have been cleared and the retaining wall built. Seating is also provided at the bottom. The Milton Mount College is now clearly visible, with its ornate, rustic wooden fence.

21966. Gravesend. Milton Mount College.

96. *Milton Mount College* was founded by Reverend William Guest, the Prince's Street Congregational church minister. It was to be established for the daughters of Congregational Church ministers and based on the Hoylake Female Seminary in the U.S.A. The site on the south-east of Windmill Hill was obtained, its location giving rise to the name Milton Mount College. Designed by C.E. Robins, a Southampton architect, the building costs were estimated at £9,750. The foundation stone was laid on 5th October 1871, by Samuel Morley M.P. Miss Selina Hadland, a very experienced and remarkable woman, was the first headmistress from 1873 to 1889. The Milton Congregational Church, opened nearby, in 1874, was close enough for the staff and pupils to attend.

Elliott & Fry,   MILTON MOUNT COLLEGE, GRAVESEND.   Dining Hall.   London, W.

97. *Milton Mount College* was originally built to accommodate 150 pupils, each with a single cubicle, except for sisters, who shared. A new wing was added in 1883, to accommodate a further 32 pupils. This view is of the ornate dining room. The college was a pioneer amongst girls schools in many things. It was the first to have domestic science, handiwork and teacher training departments, also a laboratory, gymnasium and even a school magazine. The pupils achieved high marks in exams and helped locally in a children's home, run by a Miss Sharman.

MILTON MOUNT COLLEGE
'The Carter Reading Room'

98. *The new 'Carter' reading room is shown on this card, sent in 1914.* Later that year, the pupils of Milton Mount College were involved in 'sewing and knitting parties' to help with the war effort. On 4th June 1915, a Zeppelin dropped bombs on Windmill Hill, breaking some of the college windows. It was decided to move the school to a safer area and the Royal Agricultural College at Cirencester was rented, with the school reopening there in September. Vickers, Maxim and Co. used the old college to house munitions workers. However, the Admiralty requisitioned the college as a naval hospital to treat venereal disease. This meant that, with the attached stigma and threatened staff resignations, the school did not return to Gravesend. The college became a Roman Catholic orphanage and was demolished in 1972.

ARNOLD'S FOOTPATH & BRONTE VILLAS, GRAVESEND.

5064

99. *Arnold's footpath* leads from Parrock Road to Church Walk, behind the houses of what is now Parrock Avenue. The field opposite was land owned by G.M. Arnold. The pupils of Milton Mount College used part of his meadow for sport. The villas in the distance, on the eastern slope of Windmill Hill, include Bronte Villas, now a private school.

1915.

Entrance to Barracks, Gravesend. 5.

100. *Milton Barracks'* entrance, off Wellington street, with the guardhouse on the left. The card has on the reverse 'L.W.B. quartered here Jan 1915 with 9th Queens'. Recruiting and advertising posters for the army embellish the pillars and railings. A notice on the gate pillar warns vehicles entering and leaving, to proceed at walking pace. The barracks were built in 1863 and closed in 1971. The guardhouse was demolished and the site behind it is now the new Holy Trinity School. During the 1970's, the police station was temporarily housed in the barracks, while the new police station was being built.

101. *Soldiers trench-digging in Milton Barracks*, with the perimeter wall behind, beyond which is the meadow of G.M. Arnold. The view was taken before the start of the First World War and offers a clue to the pending fate of these men. Trench warfare and all its horrors awaited them in France and Belgium.

102. *Christ Church School* in Russell Street was established in 1851. It was used for five years as a mission church until the old Christ Church was built nearby. The school was enlarged and survived until 1936. This view shows the 'Boys' Group 4' in about 1910, with their schoolmistress on the left. The 'unsmiling' boys are wearing long, laced-up boots and stockings full of holes. They all have huge collars, some of lace and others have sailors' collars.

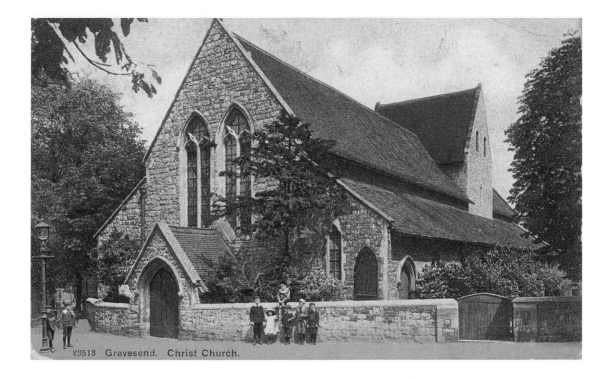

23513 Gravesend. Christ Church.

103. *The old Christ Church* was built in 1856 as a result of the increasing population in this part of Gravesend. The sale of St. John's Church to the Catholic Church may also have been a contributing factor. The church was extended and concerts were held there by soldiers from the nearby Milton Barracks. The church became unsafe and as taken down in 1932. All that remains of the old church are some blocks of stone in the centre of Christchurch Green. The church, however, was rebuilt on a site in Old Road East, the foundation stone being laid in 1934, by the Countess of Darnley.

99572 Windmill Gardens, Gravesend.

104. *Windmill Hill Gardens* were formally opened by the Lord Mayor of London in May 1902. Set out with a bowling green and tennis courts, together with ornamental gardens, they were a popular place to visit. Entertainment was organised by the Borough Fetes Committee, who arranged open-air concerts every other Wednesday evening, throughout the summer. The view in the 1920's show the bandstand with stacked chairs on the right. The bowling green is on the left and in the distance is the rear entrance to the garden of the Windmill Tavern.

21985 Gravesend, from Windmill Hill.

105. *This view from Windmill Hill* shows the Milton Congregational Church, Clarence Place, which was built in 1874, following a rift at the Prince's Street Church. The pastor, Reverend William Guest, broke away with his followers, to form this new church, which had a capacity for 750. In time, the disagreement was healed and the two churches cooperated. It survived as a church for about 80 years, closing in 1955, after which it became a warehouse and in 1968, the Sikh temple. Clarence Place used to be known as Lacey Terrace, named after the builder of the dwelling-houses.

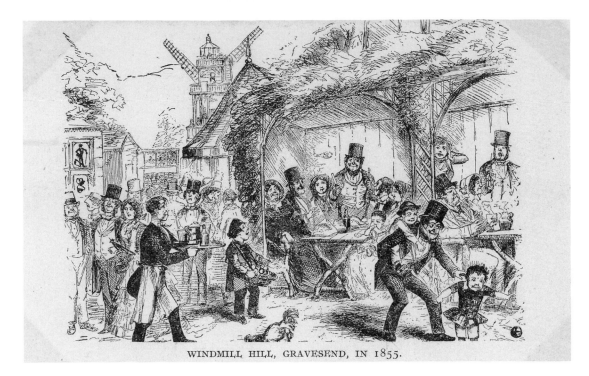

WINDMILL HILL, GRAVESEND, IN 1855.

106. *Windmill Hill* was a favourite destination for the many visitors to Gravesend. This card, issued by the Gravesend Magazine of 3 Railway Place, depicts a scene in 1855. The original article was set out in the Illustrated Times of 6 October that year and describes the view on a pleasant September afternoon. The visitors having arrived, either on the new railway or by paddle steamer, have toiled up the hill to the old windmill with its camera obscura. They have ridden donkeys, had fortunes told by gypsies and partaken of the refreshments available. The trellised booths are full of customers and children are playing with their father all enjoying their holiday.

107. *This pleasant view, entitled 'On Windmill Hill',* is of the top of Windmill Hill in 1905, with the visitors sheltering under the trees. The benches provide a cool spot away from the sun. The last windmill became unsafe and was pulled down in 1894. The old Belle Vue Hotel was burned down on Mafeking Night in 1900. The panoramic view of the surrounding countryside, town and river is still an attraction today.

108. *The War Memorial*, erected by public subscription, was unveiled in a part of Windmill Hill Gardens, facing Clarence Place in 1922. The unveiling was performed by General Lord Horne, after a service with a large number of people present. It was damaged by bombing in the last war and had to be re-erected. The memorial contains the names of the fallen of both world wars.